Sock Hop
Socks to Make Your Feet Dance

For years I have amused my knitting fingers with the endless array of textures and intricate cable patterns one can create using a single strand of yarn. I have spent countless hours wandering the aisles of any yarn shop and booth I could find, searching for the most beautiful colors and fibers I might use to highlight these textural adventures in knitting. What I was unprepared for was the sheer joy inspired by Philosopher's Wool yarns and colorways.

I met Ann and Eugene Bourgeois, owners of Philosopher's Wool, at a local craft show and was entranced by the riot of color surrounding me as I stood dumbfounded in the middle of their booth. I knew immediately that I had to prolong the excitement by bringing this depth and range of colors into my own knitting and learning the Fair Isle Simplified method of knitting at Ann's and Eugene's talented hands (see page 5). After a few quick pointers and a demonstration of the four stitches involved, I was off and knitting my way to sheer joy!

Had I been told then that I might one day write a book of sock patterns based on the beautiful sweaters created by Ann and Eugene, I would not have believed it. But when I showed Ann and Eugene my first sock knit in leftover scraps of yarn from one of their kits, they insisted, and so began the journey of what was eventually to become *Sock Hop, Socks To Make Your Feet Dance*.

You are, of course, free to use whatever fair isle knitting method you are comfortable with, however, I highly recommend their Fair Isle Simplified method. I have yet to find an easier method for knitting even fair isle. What I have presented in this book is a collection of vibrant sock patterns that coordinate beautifully with Philosopher's Wool sweaters as well as stand beautifully by themselves. The colors and lively patterns will have your feet dancing a jig in no time!

—Joseph Madl

Contents

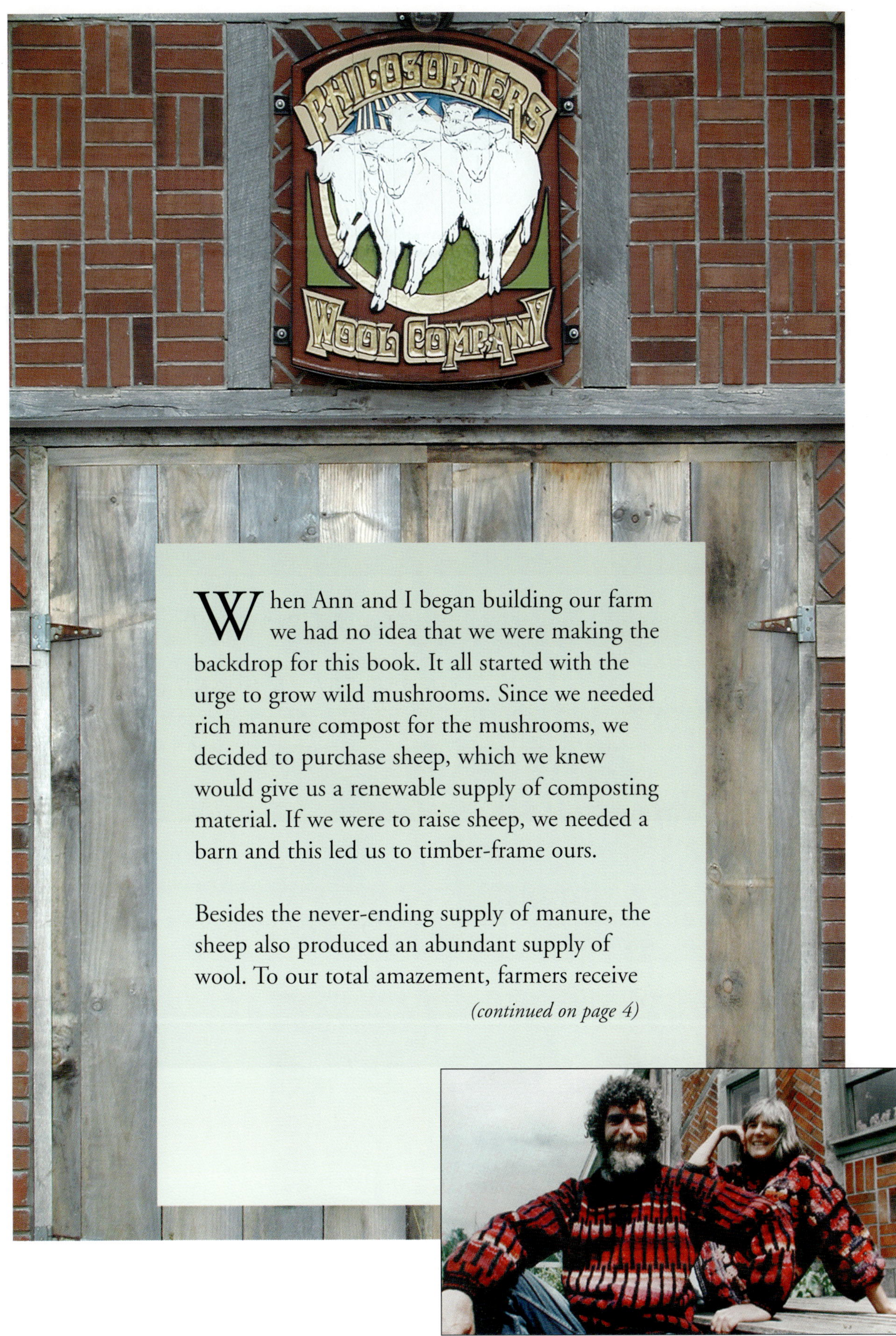

When Ann and I began building our farm we had no idea that we were making the backdrop for this book. It all started with the urge to grow wild mushrooms. Since we needed rich manure compost for the mushrooms, we decided to purchase sheep, which we knew would give us a renewable supply of composting material. If we were to raise sheep, we needed a barn and this led us to timber-frame ours.

Besides the never-ending supply of manure, the sheep also produced an abundant supply of wool. To our total amazement, farmers receive

(continued on page 4)

(continued from page 3)

next to nothing for the fleece, so we spun our fleece into beautiful yarn. Now, besides our own wool, we buy almost 5% of the fleece from local farmers.

Philosopher's wool is a name used for zinc oxide, something that alchemist's during the middle Ages discovered by accident in their quest for the philosopher's stone. Philosopher's wool (zinc oxide) has been used ever since to combat itchiness! As it turns out, our wool isn't at all itchy or picky; hence the name we selected for this company, The Philosopher's Wool Co. Our wool is 100% real wool, but without the itch. It is spun for strength and durability.

We began by designing and knitting sweaters, all the while, developing our Fair Isle techniques (see page 5). The colors we selected have been used for over 500 years—simple and in the muted colors of nature. We created groupings of colors called "colorways." Each of our colors can be used in combination with ten or more other colors. This gives us great flexibility and allows us to create patterns that look very different from one another just by changing the colorway. People are often amazed by the variety of sweaters we've created from just a few patterns. The combinations in colors account for their differences.

A friend, Joseph Madl, came to us with an idea for a book of Fair Isle socks to go with our sweaters and hats. We quickly agreed and the socks within this book were created using these unique patterns. We, of course, recommend Philosopher's wool, but any worsted weight yarn of your choosing will result in a pleasing pair of socks. Let your imagination run wild; create socks that make you want to dance! Socks that are unique to you and you alone.

So, what was once an idea for growing wild mushrooms grew into what is now the best Fair Isle design house in North America. We are very grateful to all who have helped us along the way.

—Ann and Eugene Bourgeois

Socks shown at left give samples of "colorways"—color groupings for sweater patterns created by Philosopher's Wool Co.

Two-handed Fair Isle Knitting

Knitting with right-hand color:

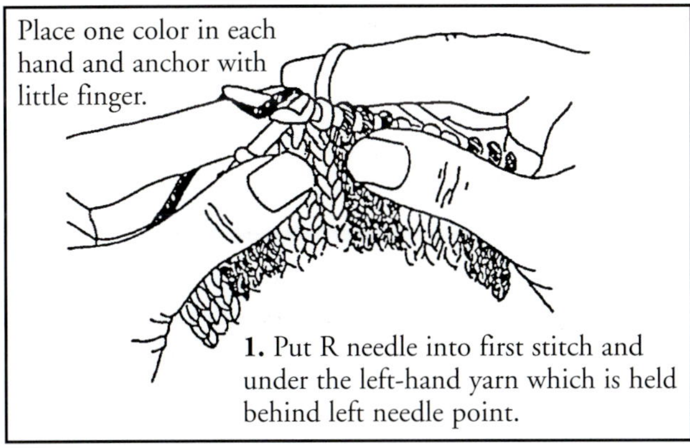

Place one color in each hand and anchor with little finger.

1. Put R needle into first stitch and under the left-hand yarn which is held behind left needle point.

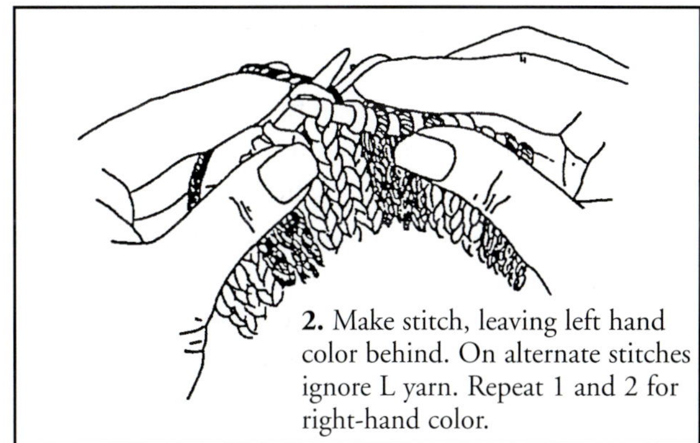

2. Make stitch, leaving left hand color behind. On alternate stitches ignore L yarn. Repeat 1 and 2 for right-hand color.

Knitting with left-hand color:

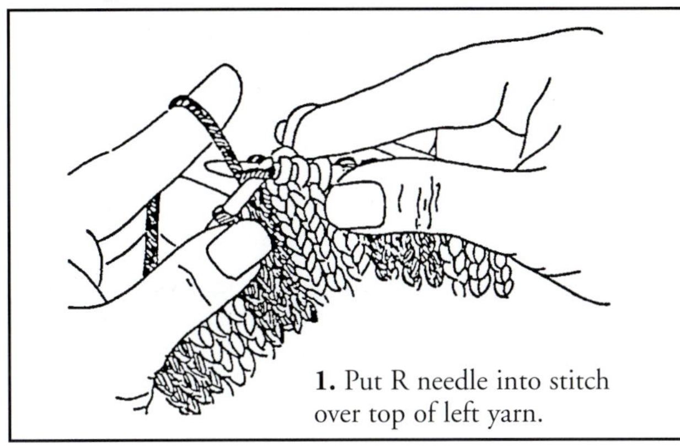

1. Put R needle into stitch over top of left yarn.

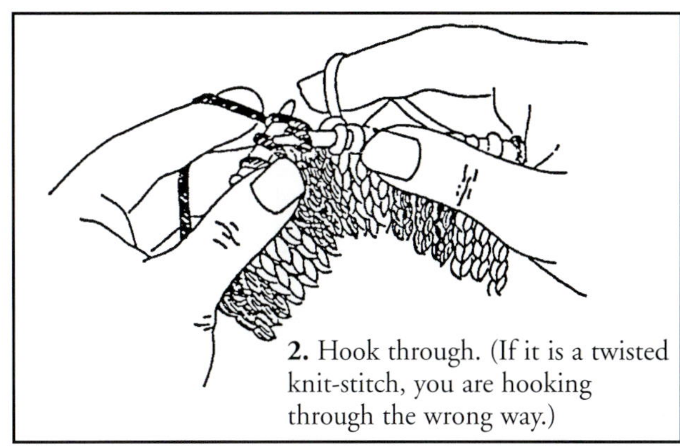

2. Hook through. (If it is a twisted knit-stitch, you are hooking through the wrong way.)

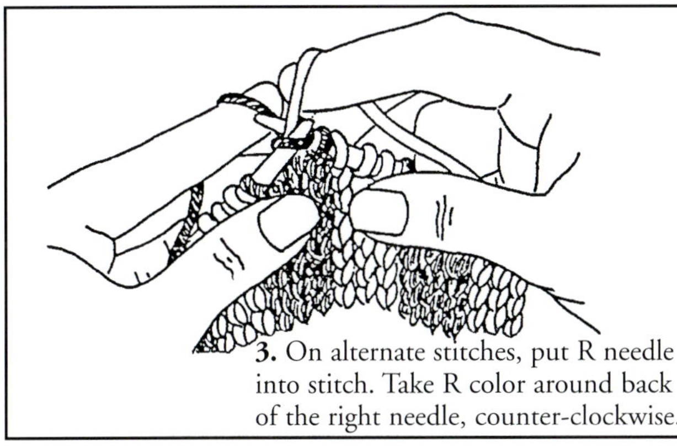

3. On alternate stitches, put R needle into stitch. Take R color around back of the right needle, counter-clockwise.

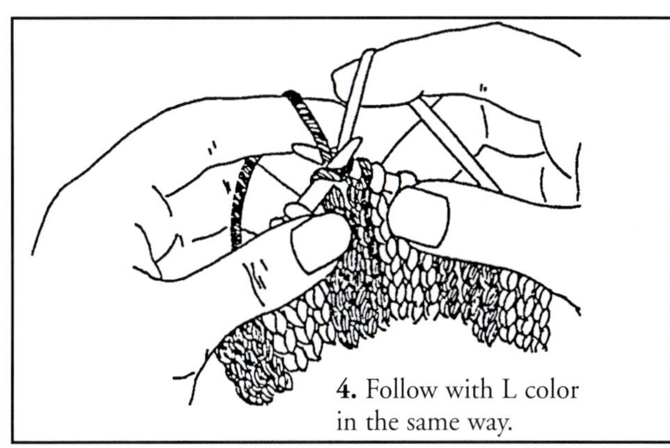

4. Follow with L color in the same way.

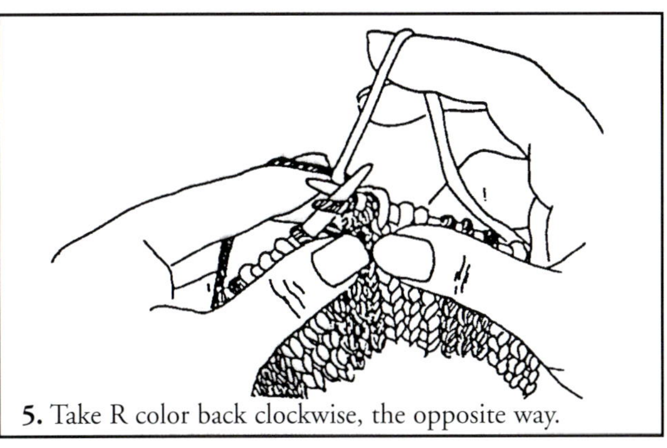

5. Take R color back clockwise, the opposite way.

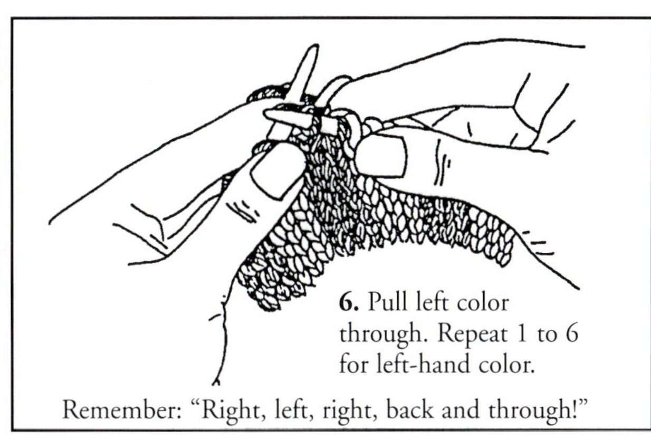

6. Pull left color through. Repeat 1 to 6 for left-hand color.

Remember: "Right, left, right, back and through!"

Basic Socks

*T*hese socks are simple to knit and great for using up left over bits of worsted wool yarn from your yarn basket. Have fun experimenting with different colors for the patterns, as well as the heels, toes, and top ribbing. Don't be afraid to vary from the pattern and find what is pleasing to your own eye.

MATERIALS

Approx. 200 grams of Philosopher's Wool worsted wool in assorted colors or equivalent

Set of 5 dpn's in 3.25 mm (or size needed to obtain gauge)

INSTRUCTIONS

Size:

Adult Small (Adult Medium)

Gauge:

5.5 stitches per inch

Cast on 48 (60) stitches and divide evenly over 4 needles.

Join without twisting, and work K3, P1 rib in random stripes of color until cuff measures 8 inches (or desired length).

Heel:

Knit to the end of Needle 1 and slip sts from Needle 4 onto Needle 1. Work the heel in one solid color (or not…play…have fun with your knitting!). With wrong side of work facing you, work back and forth across heel sts on 2 needles as follows:

Row 1: Sl1, P to end of row
Row 2: *Sl1, K1. Repeat from * to end of row.

Repeat these two rows until heel flap measures 2^1/$_2$ (2^3/$_4$) inches, ending with Row 1.

Shape Heel:

Row 1: Knit 2 sts past center, SSK, K1, turn

Row 2: Sl1, P5, P2tog, P1, turn
Row 3: Sl1, K6, SSK, K1, turn
Row 4: Sl1, P7, P2tog, P1, turn

Continue shaping heel, working 1 more st in the middle and decreasing 1 st on each row until all sts have been worked. (The dec is made with 1 st before and 1 st after the small hold on each row.) End with a Purl row.

Instep:

If using contrasting color, change back to main color. Starting with the Heel sts, knit one round, picking up and knitting 1 st for each edge st on both sides of the heel flap.

Redistribute sts so that half the heel sts are on Needle 1 and the other half are on Needle 4.

Next Round (Round A):

Needle 1: Knit to last 3 sts, K2tog, K1
Needles 2 and 3: Knit in established rib pattern
Needle 4: K1, SSK, Knit to end of needle

Next Round (Round B): Knit

Repeat these two rounds until 48 (60) sts remain.

Continue knitting rib on 2nd and 3rd (instep) needles, and knitting plain on the 1st and 4th (sole) needles until foot measures $1^1/2$ inches less than desired foot length from back of heel.

Shape Toe:

In a solid color to match the heel flap (or not…your choice):

Round 1: Knit even
Round 2:
    Needle 1 – Knit to last 3 sts, K2tog, K1
    Needle 2 – K1, SSK, knit to end
    Needle 3 – Knit to last 3 sts, K2tog, K1
    Needle 4 – K1, SSK, knit to end

Repeat last two rounds until 20 (24) sts remain. Knit one more round. Rearrange sts so you have 20 (12) sts on each of two needles (instep sts on one and heel/sole sts on the other).

Graft Toe Using Kitchener Stitch:

Cut the yarn on the front piece, leaving a long end, and thread a tapestry needle.

Work in the following sequence, pulling the yarn through as if to knit or as if to purl with even tension, and keeping yarn under points of needles to avoid tangling and extra loops.

Step 1: Purl first stitch on front needle, leave on (Fig. 1).
Step 2: Knit first stitch on back needle, leave on (Fig. 2).
Step 3: Knit first stitch on front needle, slip off.
Step 4: Purl next stitch on front needle leave on.
Step 5: Purl first stitch on back needle, slip off.
Step 6: Knit next stitch on back needle, leave on.
Repeat Steps 3–6 across until all stitches have been worked off the needles.

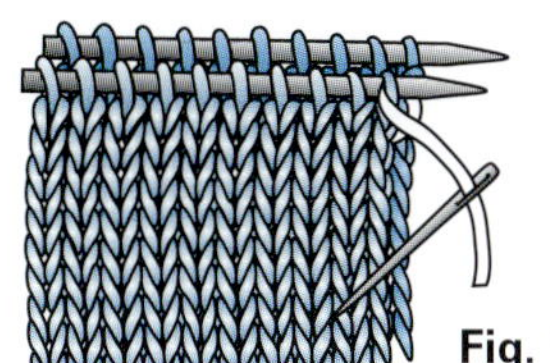

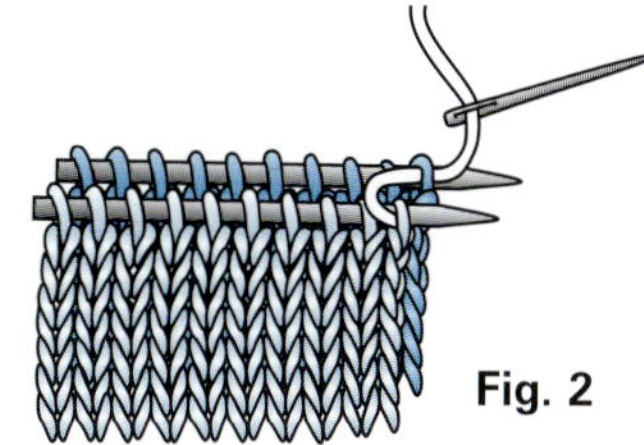

Squares Around Socks

Size:

Adult Small (Adult Medium)

Gauge:

5.5 stitches per inch

Cast on 48 (60) stitches and divide evenly over 4 needles.

Join without twisting, and work 2 inches (or desired length) of K1, P1 rib in random stripes of colors.

Begin Cuff Pattern Stitch and work until cuff measures 7 to 8 inches (or desired length), ending with a completed "square."

Heel:

Work as in Basic Sock (see page 6) using one solid color that contrasts with the squares adjoining it.

Instep:

Starting with the Heel sts, knit one round (remembering to join and change yarn colors as you work through the squares on the instep sts), picking up and knitting 1 st for each edge st on both sides of the heel flap.

Redistribute sts so that half the heel sts are on Needle 1 and the other half are on Needle 4, placing markers after the 12th (15th) st on Needle 1 and 12 (15) sts from the end of Needle 4. The sts on the outside of these markers (i.e., at the end of Needle 1 and the beginning of Needle 4) are your gussets and will be knit in a solid color (they will be knit in the yarn color that you are carrying for the square next to the gusset).

When knitting the sole sts, work the Sole Pattern Stitch on Needles 1 and 4 (taking care to knit the gusset sts in the appropriate solid color), as follows:

Next Round (Round A):

Needle 1: Knit in the Sole Pattern Stitch to the marker, then the gusset color to last 3 sts, K2tog, K1
Needles 2 and 3: Knit in established Cuff Pattern Stitch
Needle 4: In the gusset color, K1, SSK, knit to the marker, then knit in the Sole Stitch Pattern to the end

Next Round (Round B):

Needle 1: Knit in the Sole Pattern Stitch to the marker, then the gusset color to end
Needles 2 and 3: Knit in established Cuff Pattern Stitch
Needle 4: In the gusset color to the marker, then knit in the Sole Stitch Pattern to the end

Continue Sole Pattern Stitch and working decreases (on every alternate round) on Needle 1 and Needle 4 and working the Cuff Pattern Stitch on Needles 2 and 3 until 48 (60) sts remain and are divided evenly over the needles. You will no longer have any gusset sts and will therefore now work the Sole Pattern Stitch for every stitch on Needles 1 and 4.

Work instep for desired length of foot minus 1$^{1}/_{2}$ inches.

Shape Toe:

Work in same color as the Heel Flap and knit as in Basic Sock.

Graft Toe Using Kitchener Stitch:

See page 7.

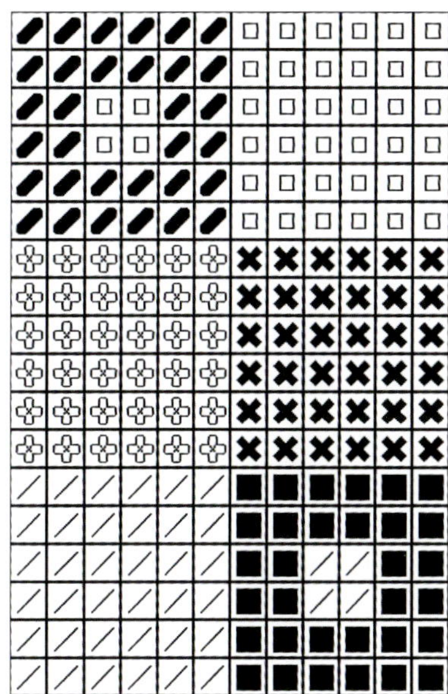

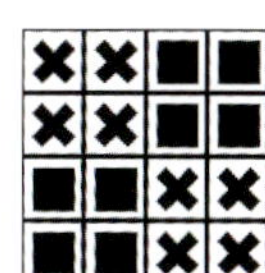

Cuff Pattern Stitch **Sole Pattern Stitch**

Alligator Teeth Socks

MATERIALS

Approx. 200 grams of Philosopher's Wool worsted wool in assorted colors or equivalent

Set of 5 dpn's in 3.25 mm (or size needed to obtain gauge)

INSTRUCTIONS

Size:
Adult Small (Adult Medium)

Gauge:
5.5 stitches per inch

Cast On 48 (60) stitches and divide evenly over 4 needles. Work 2 inches (or desired length) of K1, P1 rib in random stripes of colors. Begin Cuff Pattern Stitch and work until cuff measures 7 (8) inches (or desired length), alternately changing the background and foreground colors every 2 or 3 rounds.

Heel:
Work as in Basic Sock (see page 6) in one solid color.

Instep:
Starting with the Heel sts, knit one round in background color, picking up and knitting 1 st for each edge st on both sides of the heel flap. Redistribute sts so that half the heel sts are on Needle 1 and the other half are on Needle 4.

Work Decrease Rounds (Round A and B) as in Basic Sock. Continue working decreases (on every alternate round) on Needle 1 and Needle 4 until 48 (60) sts remain and are divided evenly over the needles.

Work instep for desired length of foot minus $2^{1}/_{2}$ inches.

Work one repeat of Cuff Pattern Stitch, alternately changing foreground and background colors every 2 or 3 rounds as in cuff.

Toe:
Work as in Basic Sock in solid color.

Graft Toe Using Kitchener Stitch:
See page 7.

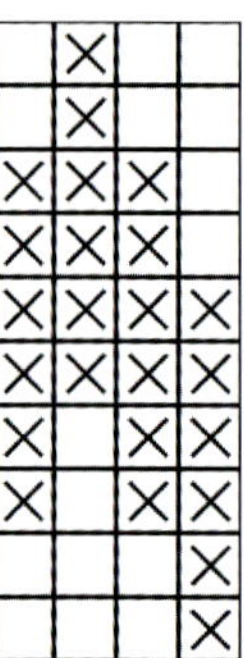

Cuff Pattern Stitch

The Alligator Teeth Socks, as written, have a solid instep and sole. Note how you can vary your socks for a totally new look by simply adding one of the Sole Pattern Stitches as in the photo opposite. There is no end to the wonderful combinations you can create!

Garden Patch Socks

MATERIALS

Approx. 200 grams of Philosopher's Wool worsted wool in assorted colors or equivalent

Set of 5 dpn's in 3.25 mm (or size needed to obtain gauge)

INSTRUCTIONS

Size:

Adult Small (Adult Medium)

Gauge:

5.5 stitches per inch

Cast On 48 (60) stitches and divide evenly over 4 needles. Work 2 inches (or desired length) of K1, P1 rib in random stripes of colors. Begin Cuff Pattern Stitch and work until cuff measures 7 (8) inches (or desired length), alternately changing the background and foreground colors every 2 or 3 rounds.

Heel:

Work as in Basic Sock (see page 6) in one solid color.

Instep:

Starting with the Heel sts, knit in same color as heel one round, picking up and knitting 1 st for each edge st on both sides of the heel flap. Redistribute sts so that half the heel sts are on Needle 1 and the other half are on Needle 4.

Work Decrease Rounds (Round A and B) as in Basic Sock. Continue working decreases (on every alternate round) on Needle 1 and Needle 4 until 48 (60) sts remain and are divided evenly over the needles.

Work instep for desired length of foot minus 2 1/4 inches.

Work Toe Band Chart, with background in same color as instep.

Toe:

Work as in Basic Sock in same color as heel and instep.

Graft Toe Using Kitchener Stitch:

See page 7.

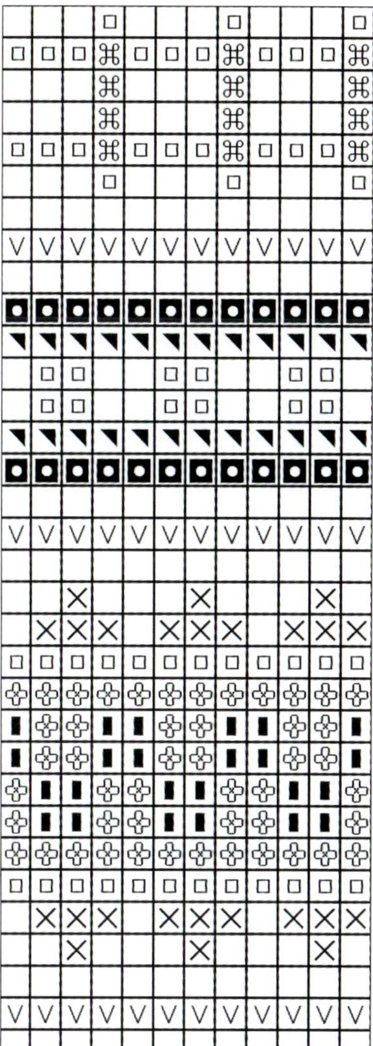

Cuff Pattern Stitch

$\boxed{V}$ **Purl in a contrasting color**

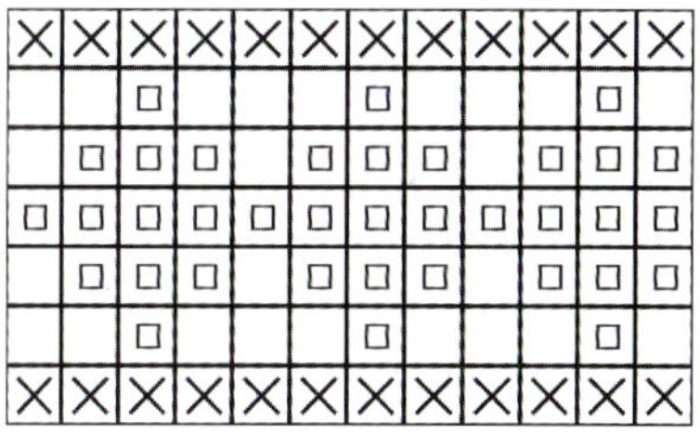

Toe Band

Color Your Own Socks

MATERIALS

Approx. 200 grams of Philosopher's Wool worsted wool in assorted colors or equivalent

Set of 5 dpn's in 3.25 mm (or size needed to obtain gauge)

INSTRUCTIONS

Size:

Adult Small (Adult Medium)

Gauge:

5.5 stitches per inch

Cast On 48 (60) stitches and divide evenly over 4 needles. Work 2 inches (or desired length) of K1, P1 rib in random stripes of colors or in one solid color (your choice). Begin Cuff Pattern Stitch and work one complete set of all rounds.

Heel:

Work as in Basic Sock (see page 6).

Instep:

Starting with the Heel sts, knit one round (in the color you just finished turning your heel flap with), picking up and knitting 1 st for each edge st on both sides of the heel flap. Redistribute sts so that half the heel sts are on Needle 1 and the other half are on Needle 4.

Work Decrease Rounds (Round A and B) as in Basic Sock. Continue working decreases (on every alternate round) on Needle 1 and Needle 4 until 48 (60) sts remain and are divided evenly over the needles.

Work instep for desired length of foot minus 2^{1}/4 inches.

Work the Toe Band Chart.

Work Toe as in Basic Sock, in a solid color to match the heel flap.

Graft Toe Using Kitchener Stitch:

See page 7.

Now go knit the second sock!

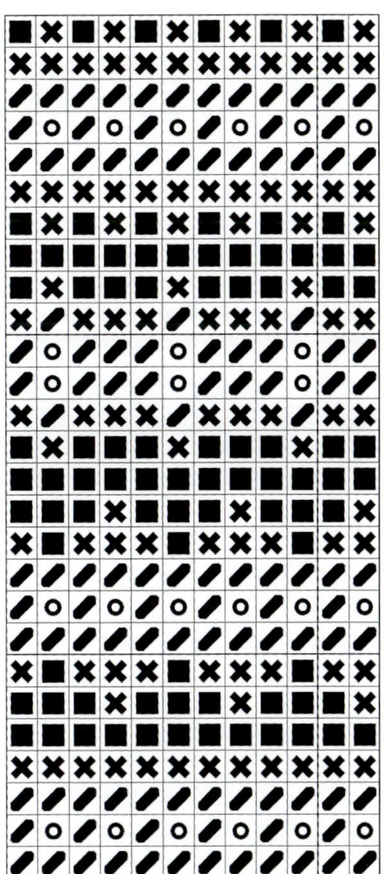

Cuff Pattern Stitch

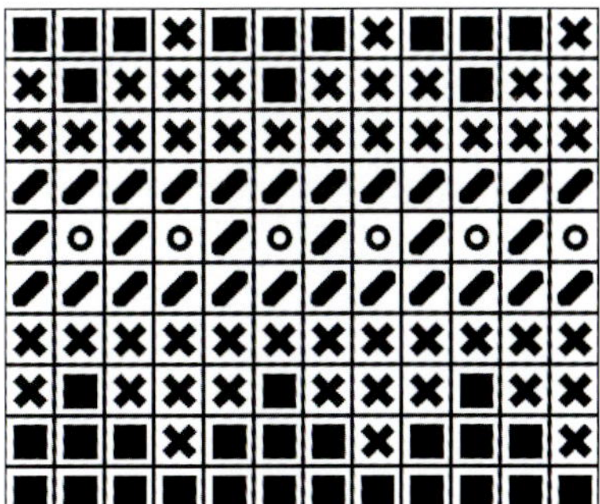

Toe Band

Fractured Diamonds Socks

MATERIALS

Approx. 200 grams of Philosopher's Wool worsted wool in assorted colors or equivalent

Set of 5 dpn's in 3.25 mm (or size needed to obtain gauge)

INSTRUCTIONS

Size:

Adult Small (Adult Medium)

Gauge:

5.5 stitches per inch

Cast On 48 (60) stitches and divide evenly over 4 needles. Work rounds 1 through 8 of chart over K2, P2 rib for $1^1/2$ to 2 inches (ending with round 4 or 8). Knit rounds 9 through 14 once. Knit and repeat rounds 15 through 20 until cuff measures 6 to 8 inches (or desired length), ending with round 17 or 20.

Heel:

Work as in Basic Sock (see page 6) in one solid color.

Instep:

Starting with the Heel sts, knit one round (in the color you just finished turning your heel flap with), picking up and knitting 1 st for each edge st on both sides of the heel flap. Redistribute sts so that half the heel sts are on Needle 1 and the other half are on Needle 4.

Work Decrease Rounds (Round A and B) as in Basic Sock. Continue working decreases (on every alternate round) on Needle 1 and Needle 4 until 48 (60) sts remain and are divided evenly over the needles.

Work instep for desired length of foot minus $2^1/4$ inches. Work rounds 15 through 20 from chart.

Toe:

Work as in Basic Sock in a solid color.

Graft Toe Using Kitchener Stitch:

See page 7.

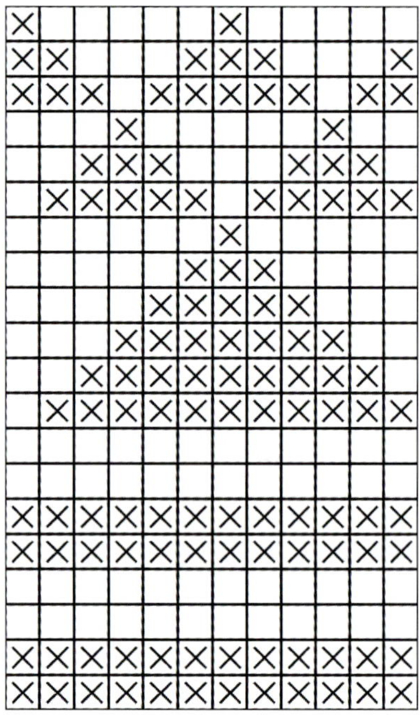

For a more lively and colorful pair of socks, try changing the foreground color with each new triangle round (every three rounds). Or even change both the background and foreground colors for each set of triangles!

Timber Frame Socks

MATERIALS

Approx. 200 grams of Philosopher's Wool worsted wool in assorted colors or equivalent

Set of 5 dpn's in 3.25 mm (or size needed to obtain gauge)

INSTRUCTIONS

Size:

Adult Small (Adult Medium)

Gauge:

5.5 stitches per inch

Cast On 48 (60) stitches and divide evenly over 4 needles. Work 2 inches (or desired length) of K1, P1 rib in random stripes of colors. Begin Cuff Pattern Stitch and work until cuff measures 7 (8) inches (or desired length), alternately changing the background color every 2 or 3 rounds, but leaving the foreground (or vertical stripes) in one solid color.

Heel:

Work as in Basic Sock (see page 6) in one solid color.

Instep:

Starting with the Heel sts, knit one round, joining and knitting with the foreground color for the vertical stripes across the instep sts (following the chart where you left off before beginning heel), and picking up 1 st for each edge st on both sides of the heel flap. Redistribute sts so that half the heel sts are on Needle 1 and the other half are on Needle 4. You will be working the instep sts by continuing to follow the Pattern Stitch Chart and the gusset and sole sts in seed stitch (i.e., knit 1 st in foreground color then one st in background color and repeat).

Work Decrease Rounds (Round A and B) as in Basic Sock. Continue working decreases (on every alternate round) on Needle 1 and Needle 4 until 48 (60) sts remain and are divided evenly over the needles.

Work instep for desired length of foot minus 1½ inches.

Toe:

Work as in Basic Sock in solid color.

Graft Toe Using Kitchener Stitch:

See page 7.

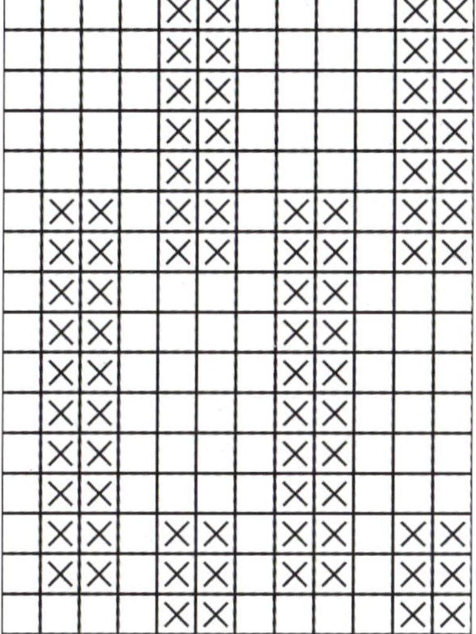

This pattern lends itself to many wonderful color combinations and variations. For a more subtle Timber Frame Pattern, try changing the foreground color every 2 or 3 rounds as well. This creates a softer design that is delightful!

Tradition Socks

MATERIALS

Approx. 200 grams of Philosopher's Wool worsted wool in assorted colors or equivalent

Set of 5 dpn's in 3.25 mm (or size needed to obtain gauge)

INSTRUCTIONS

Size:

Adult Small (Adult Medium)

Gauge:

5.5 stitches per inch

Cast On 48 (60) stitches and divide evenly over 4 needles. Work 2 inches (or desired length) of K1, P1 rib in random stripes of colors or in one solid color (your choice). Begin Cuff Pattern Stitch and work one complete set of all rounds.

Heel:

Work as in Basic Sock (see page 6) in random stripes to coordinate/match the rib, or in one solid color.

Instep:

Starting with the Heel sts, knit one round, picking up and knitting 1 st for each edge st on both sides of the heel flap.

Redistribute sts so that half the heel sts are on Needle 1 and the other half are on Needle 4, placing markers after the 12th (15th) st on Needle 1 and 12 (15) sts from the end of Needle 4. The sts on the outside of these markers (i.e., at the end of Needle 1 and the beginning of Needle 4) are your gussets and will be knit in a solid color.

Join the second color for the Instep Pattern Stitch and work the Sole Stitch Pattern on Needles 1 and 4 (taking care to knit the gusset stitches in a solid color), following the directions below:

Next Round (Round A):

Needle 1: Knit to last 3 sts, K2tog, K1
Needles 2 and 3: Work in Instep Pattern Stitch
Needle 4: K1, SSK, Knit to end of needle

Next Round (Round B):

Needle 1: Knit
Needles 2 and 3: Work in Instep Pattern Stitch
Needle 4: Knit

Continue Sole Pattern Stitch and working decreases (on every alternate round) on Needle 1 and Needle 4 and working the Instep Pattern Stitch on Needles 2 and 3 until 48 (60) sts remain and are divided evenly over the

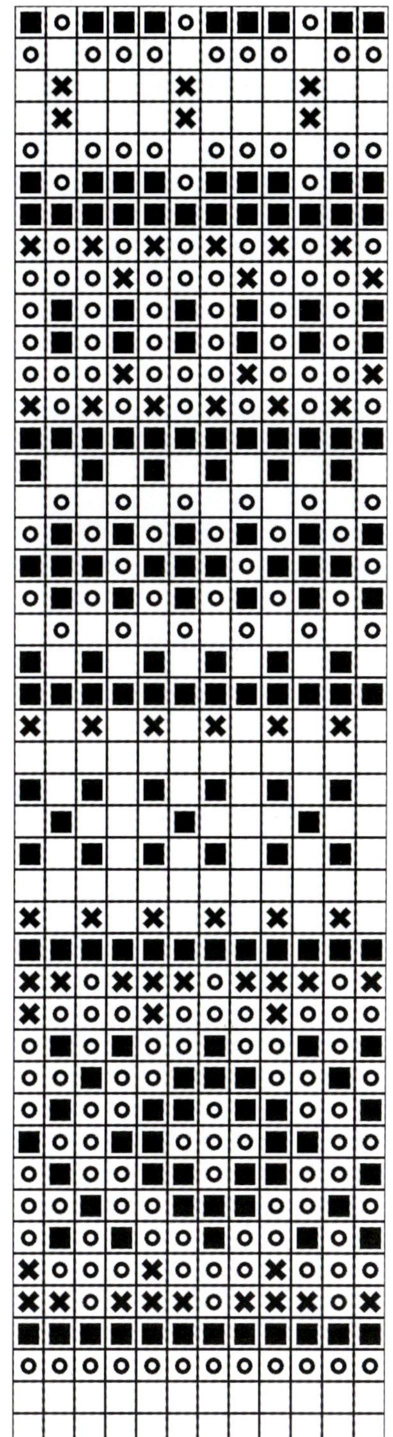

needles. You will no longer have any gusset stitches and will therefore now work the Sole Pattern Stitch for every stitch on Needles 1 and 4.

Work instep for desired length of foot minus $1^1/2$ inches.

Toe:

Work as in Basic Sock in random color stripes to coordinate with the cuff and heel flap or in a solid color.

Graft Toe Using Kitchener Stitch:

See page 7.

Cuff Pattern Stitch

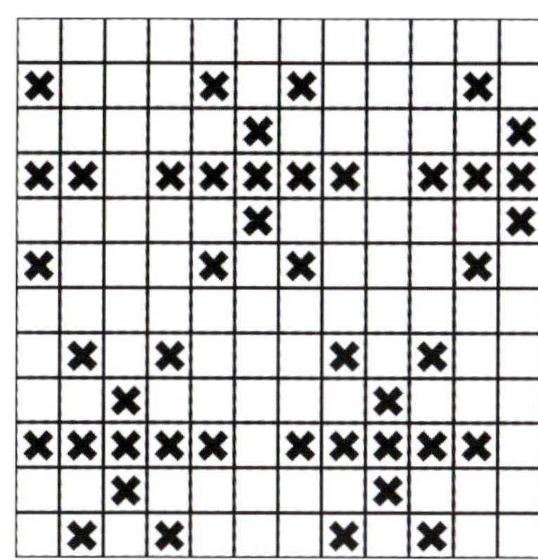

Instep Pattern Stitch

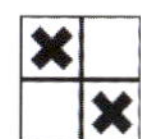

Sole Pattern Stitch

Kilim Socks

MATERIALS

Approx. 200 grams of Philosopher's Wool worsted wool in assorted colors or equivalent

Set of 5 dpn's in 3.25 mm (or size needed to obtain gauge)

INSTRUCTIONS

Size:

Adult Small (Adult Medium)

Gauge:

5.5 stitches per inch

Cast On 48 (60) stitches and divide evenly over 4 needles. Work 2 inches (or desired length) of K1, P1 rib in random stripes of colors. Begin Cuff Pattern Stitch and work until cuff measures 7 (8) inches (or desired length), alternately changing the background and foreground colors every 2 or 3 rounds.

Heel:

Work as in Basic Sock (see page 6) in one solid color.

Instep:

Starting with the Heel sts, knit one round (in the color you just finished turning your heel flap with), picking up and knitting 1 st for each edge st on both sides of the heel flap. Redistribute sts so that half the heel sts are on Needle 1 and the other half are on Needle 4.

Work Decrease Rounds (Round A and B) as in Basic Sock. Continue working decreases (on every alternate round) on Needle 1 and Needle 4 until 48 (60) sts remain and are divided evenly over the needles.

Work instep for desired length of foot minus $2^{1/4}$ inches.

Work Toe Band Chart, changing color in foreground stitches at least three times and leaving the background color the same as the heel/instep color.

Toe:

Work as in Basic Sock in solid color.

Graft Toe Using Kitchener Stitch:

See page 7.

Option:

Use a contrasting color for the heel and toe background colors to set them off nicely!

Toe Band

Cuff Pattern Stitch

Stars Socks

MATERIALS

Approx. 200 grams of Philosopher's Wool worsted wool in assorted colors or equivalent

Set of 5 dpn's in 3.25 mm (or size needed to obtain gauge)

INSTRUCTIONS

Size:

Adult Small (Adult Medium)

Gauge:

5.5 stitches per inch

Cast On 48 (60) stitches and divide evenly over 4 needles. Work 2 inches (or desired length) of K1, P1 rib in random stripes of colors. Begin Cuff Pattern Stitch and work until cuff measures 7 (8) inches (or desired length). When working the Cuff Pattern, alternately change star and background colors every two or three rounds.

Heel:

Work as in Basic Sock (see page 6).

Instep:

Starting with the Heel sts, knit one round (in the background color you just finished turning your heel flap with), picking up and knitting 1 st for each edge st on both sides of the heel flap. Redistribute sts so that half the heel sts are on Needle 1 and the other half are on Needle 4.

Work Decrease Rounds (Round A and B) as in Basic Sock. Continue working decreases (on every alternate round) on Needle 1 and Needle 4 until 48 (60) sts remain and are divided evenly over the needles.

Optional:

Carry the star chart from cuff down along the instep and sole, knitting solid background color in for gussets (as in Tradition Socks).

Work instep for desired length of foot minus $1^3/4$ inches.

Work Toe Band Chart, changing color in stars once.

Toe:

Work as in Basic Sock in random stripes or in one solid color.

Graft Toe Using Kitchener Stitch:

See page 7.

You can vary this pattern beautifully by working the sole and instep in contrasting colors (as in the photo) simply by carrying the yarn not in use, being careful to weave each stitch so as not to create long floats, or by carrying the stars from the cuff down along the instep and knitting one of the sole patterns stitches elsewhere in the book for the sole.

Rainbows Socks

MATERIALS

Approx. 200 grams of Philosopher's Wool worsted wool in assorted colors or equivalent

Set of 5 dpn's in 3.25 mm (or size needed to obtain gauge)

INSTRUCTIONS

Size:

Adult Small (Adult Medium)

Gauge:

5.5 stitches per inch

Cast On 48 (60) stitches and divide evenly over 4 needles. Work 2 inches (or desired length) of K1, P1 rib in random stripes of colors. Begin Cuff Pattern Stitch and work until cuff measures 7 (8) inches (or desired length), alternately changing the background color every 2 or 3 rounds, but leaving the foreground (or vertical stripes) in one solid color.

Heel:

Work as in Basic Sock (see page 6) in one solid color.

Instep:

Starting with the Heel sts, knit one round, joining and knitting with the foreground color for the vertical stripes across the instep sts (following the chart where you left off before beginning heel), and picking up 1 st for each edge st on both sides of the heel flap. Redistribute sts so that half the heel sts are on Needle 1 and the other half are on Needle 4. You will be working the instep sts by continuing to follow the Pattern Stitch Chart and the gusset and sole sts in seed stitch (i.e., knit 1 st in foreground color then one st in background color and repeat).

Work Decrease Rounds (Round A and B) as in Basic Sock. Continue working decreases (on every alternate round) on Needle 1 and Needle 4 until 48 (60) sts remain and are divided evenly over the needles.

Work instep for desired length of foot minus 1^1/2 inches.

Toe:

Work as in Basic Sock in solid color.

Graft Toe Using Kitchener Stitch:

See page 7.

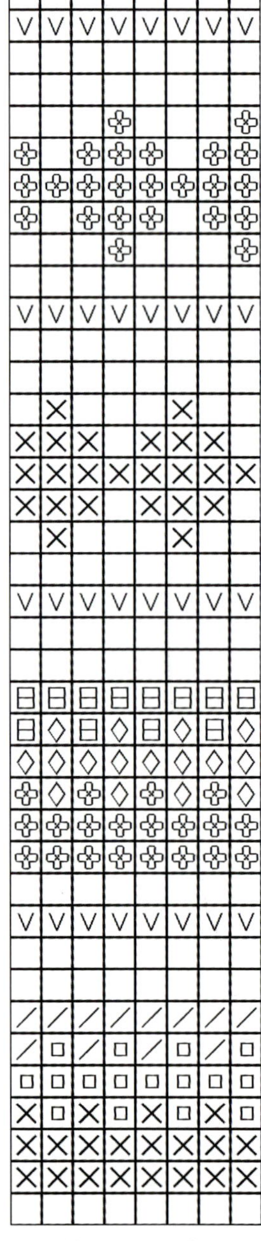

Cuff Pattern Stitch

Trillium Socks

MATERIALS

Approx. 200 grams of Philosopher's Wool worsted wool in assorted colors or equivalent

Set of 5 dpn's in 3.25 mm (or size needed to obtain gauge)

INSTRUCTIONS

Size:

Adult Small (Adult Medium)

Gauge:

5.5 stitches per inch

Cast On 48 (60) stitches and divide evenly over 4 needles. Work 2 inches (or desired length) of K1, P1 rib in random stripes of colors. Begin Cuff Pattern Stitch and work until cuff measures 7 (8) inches (or desired length), alternately changing the background and foreground colors every 2 or 3 rounds.

Heel:

Work as in Basic Sock (see page 6) in one solid color.

Instep:

(May be knit in one solid background color OR in random stripes.) Starting with the Heel sts, knit one round in background color, picking up and knitting 1 st for each edge st on both sides of the heel flap. Redistribute sts so that half the heel sts are on Needle 1 and the other half are on Needle 4.

Work Decrease Rounds (Round A and B) as in Basic Sock. Continue working decreases (on every alternate round) on Needle 1 and Needle 4 until 48 (60) sts remain and are divided evenly over the needles.

Work instep for desired length of foot minus 2$^{1}/_{2}$ inches.

Work one repeat of Toe Band Pattern Stitch, alternately changing foreground and background colors every 2 or 3 rounds as in cuff.

Toe:

Work as in Basic Sock in solid color.

Graft Toe Using Kitchener Stitch:

See page 7.

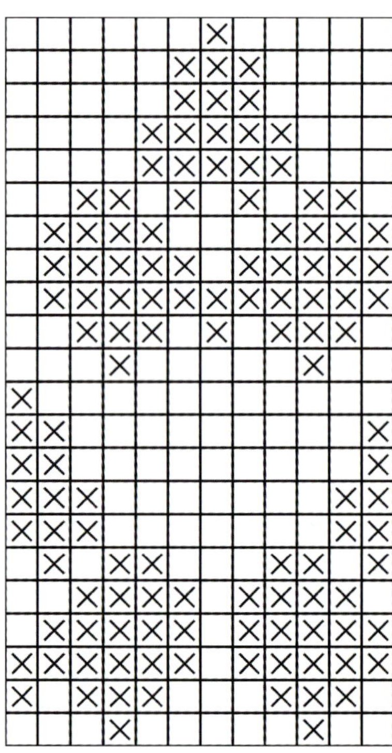

For an elegant look, carry the pattern stitch down the instep, using seed or other Sole Pattern Stitch on the sole stitches, as in the photo opposite.

Circus Socks

MATERIALS

Approx. 200 grams of Philosopher's Wool worsted wool in assorted colors or equivalent

Set of 5 dpn's in 3.25 mm (or size needed to obtain gauge)

INSTRUCTIONS

Size:

Adult Small (Adult Medium)

Gauge:

5.5 stitches per inch

Single Braid:

Step 1: Work one round using two colors as follows: *K1 in color A, K1 in color B, repeat from * until the end of the round.

Step 2: Brings both colors to front as if to purl. P1 with color A, * bring color B from the FRONT under color A and up, P1, bring color A from the FRONT under color B and P1, repeat from * to the end of the round being careful to always twist in the same direction. The yarn will be twisting in a counter-clockwise direction with each stitch and will become twisted. Keep pushing the twist away from yourself.

Step 3: To complete a single braid, it is necessary to untwist the yarn. To do this, push the knitting well back from the needle points. Hold the work up and allow the work to dangle and spin until the twist is eliminated.

Double Braid:

Step 1: Same as Single Braid
Step 2: Same as Single Braid
Step 3: P1 in color A. * Bring color B from the BACK under color A (that is, in the opposite direction as in Step 2) and P1, bring color A from the BACK under color B and P1. Repeat from * to the end of the round, being careful to always twist in the same direction. The yarn will be twisting in a counter-clockwise direction with each

stitch and will by the end of the round untangle completely the twists created in Step 2.

Garter Bands:

Step 1: Knit round in one color.
Step 2: Purl round in same color.

Cast On 48 (60) stitches and divide evenly over 4 needles. Work 2 inches (or desired length) of K1, P1 rib in random stripes of colors. Begin knitting random groupings of Single and Double Braids and Garter Bands for 2¹/2 to 3 inches. Work three full repeats of Diamonds Stitch Chart. Knit random groupings of Single and Double Braids and Garter Bands for 2¹/2 to 3 inches.

Heel:

Work as in Basic Sock (see page 6) in one solid color.

Instep:

Starting with the Heel sts, knit one round (in the background color used in the Diamonds Stitch area above), picking up and knitting 1 st for each edge st on both sides of the heel flap and joining the contrast color at Needle 2, knitting the Diamonds Stitch Chart across all instep sts on Needles 2 and 3. Redistribute sts so that half the heel sts are on Needle 1 and the other half are on Needle 4. Work all gusset stitches in background color. Carry contrast color all the way across all sole sts.

Work Decrease Rounds (Round A and B) as in Basic Sock. Continue working decreases (on every alternate round) on Needle 1 and Needle 4 until 48 (60) sts remain and are divided evenly over the needles.

Work instep for desired length of foot minus 1¹/2 inches.

Toe:

Work as in Basic Sock in a solid color.

Graft Toe Using Kitchener Stitch:

See page 7.

Cuff Pattern Stitch

Rose's Hose

By Rose Singerman

A few years ago the pipe major from the Kincardine, Ontario pipe band approached Rose Singerman to make traditional Aran kilt hose. She researched the design possibilities and started knitting custom fitted socks. More than 150 pairs later there are many pipers in Southern Ontario who have the luxury of performing in these gorgeous and ever so comfortable socks. A few weeks ago, I, too, was the surprised and grateful recipient of a pair of these lovely socks! Now, for the first time, there is a pattern for you, too, to knit these for appreciative feet.

MATERIALS

Approx. 250 grams of Philosopher's Wool 3-ply worsted wool

Set of 5 dpn's in 3.25 mm (or size needed to obtain gauge)

INSTRUCTIONS

Size:

Adult Large

Gauge:

5.5 stitches per inch

Cuff Pattern Stitch:

Rnd 1: Purl
Rnd 2: *K3tog, M3, rep from *
Rnd 3: Purl
Rnd 4: *M3, K3tog, rep from *

NOTE: M3 = Make 3 sts by K1, P1, K1 into same st

Cable Pattern Stitch:

Rnds 1–4: *K1, P3, K6, P3, K1, P1, rep from *
Rnd 5:   *K1, P3, C6F, P3, K1, P1, rep from *
Rnds 6–10: Repeat Rnds 1–4

NOTE: C6F = Slip 3 sts onto cable needle and hold to front, K3, K3 from cable needle

Cast On 76 sts and divide evenly over 4 needles. Knit 2 rounds of K1, P1 rib.

Knit Cuff Pattern Stitch for 3$^{1}/_{2}$ inches. Turn cuff inside out. (You will now be knitting in the opposite direction and will be looking at the wrong side of the cuff, but the right side of your new knitting).

Knit 1$^{1}/_{2}$ inches of K1, P1 rib. Decrease one stitch at the end of the last row.

Knit 7 repeats of Cable Pattern Stitch. Over next 1 repeat of Cable Pattern Stitch, decrease evenly 7 sts in each repeat, placing the decreased stitches in the purled background sts on either side of the cables. Over the next 3 repeats of Cable Pattern Stitch, decrease evenly 6 sts in each repeat, in the same manner. You should now have 50 sts on your needles. Be sure that half the sts are on Needles 1 and 4 and the other half are on Needles 2 and 3. Rearrange, if necessary.

Heel:

Work as in Basic Sock (see page 6), making the heel flap 2$^{3}/_{4}$ inches long.

Instep:

Starting with the Heel sts, knit one round, picking up and knitting 1 st for each edge st on both sides of the heel flap and knitting in the established Cable Pattern Stitch on the instep stitches on Needles 2 and 3. Redistribute sts so that half the heel sts are on Needle 1 and the other half are on Needle 4.

Work Decrease Rounds (Round A and B) as in Basic Sock, remembering to knit in established Cable Pattern Stitch on instep sts. Continue working decreases (on every alternate round) on Needle 1 and Needle 4 until 50 sts remain and are divided evenly over the needles.

Work instep for desired length of foot minus 2$^{1}/_{4}$ inches.

Work Toe as in Basic Sock.

Graft Toe Using Kitchener Stitch:

See page 7.

Conversions

Converting From One Gauge to Another:

To use yarns other than Philosopher's Wool in various weights, follow the simple conversion method below:

Knit a gauge swatch with the yarn and needles you would like to use. Carefully measure your gauge (stitches per inch). Write the gauge of your swatch below:

A. Stitches / 4 inches _________

Write the gauge of the pattern you want to convert below:

B. Stitches / 4 inches __________

Stitch Conversion:

Divide **A** by **B** and write the result here ___________. Use this result to multiply the stitches given in the pattern.

Conversion Example:

Stitches: Your swatch has 36 stitches / 4 inches but the pattern is for 22 stitches / 4 inches. Divide 36 by 22 which results in 1.6. The pattern says to cast on 60 stitches. You multiply that by 1.6 and get 96 stitches. Cast on the number of stitches closest to 96 stitches that is divisible by 12 (or however many stitches are in a full repeat of the pattern chart). In this example, you would cast on 96 stitches.

When decreasing for the toe, use a similar ratio. Using the example above, you are casting on approximately $1/3$ more stitches than the original pattern called for. Therefore, you would decrease the toe until you have $1/3$ more stitches as well. In this case, until you have 32 stitches remaining. Then graft as usual. This number is far more flexible than the cast on quantity as you may adjust the toe to suit you personal taste.

Resources

Philosopher's Wool
Inverhuron, Ontario
Canada N0G 2T0
519-368-5354
Yarn, kits, patterns
Two-handed Fair Isle Knitting Video
www.philosopherswool.com
philosophers@bmts.com

Joseph "The Sockguy" Madl
5014 Danford Dr. #4
Billings, MT 59106
406-860-4981
thesockguy@yahoo.com

Acknowledgements

Special thanks to Ann and Eugene Bourgeois for their belief in my ideas and talents and to my parents for putting up with all the madness brought into their lives while creating this book.

Many thanks to all of the Philosopher's talented knitters for creating the lovely garments that are included in this book: Jessie Andersen, Barb Carter, Flo Fischer, Ingrid Goetz, Tatiana Jacenko, Sheree Kelly, Janice Love, Pauline McMichael, Vera Portice, Shirley Purdie, Rose Singerman, Wendy Sloman, Alice Van de Klippe, Grace Veltkamp and Eileen Walker.

Many thanks also to the models who gave life to the socks and sweaters by wearing them: Eugene Bourgeois, the Bryant Family, Dawn Chang, Anne Hierlihy, Tammy Martens, Annika Van Veen, Noah Van Veen, and Watson Morris.

Many thanks to the photographer, Ann Bourgeois, and to Timber Venard for the photo on page 3.